AT THE
SCENE OF THE CRIME

WITHDRAWN

wittenberg
UNIVERSITY
THOMAS LIBRARY

EDUCATORS PUBLISHING SERVICE
Cambridge and Toronto

© 2008 by School Specialty, Inc.

Series Authors: Kay Kovalevs and Alison Dewsbury
Commissioning Editors: Rachel Elliott, Tom Beran, Lynn Robbins,
and Laura Woollett
Text by Meredith Costain
Edited by Philip Bryan and Marcy Gilbert
Designed by Regine Abos
Photographic research by Marg Barber

Making Connections® developed by School Specialty, Inc. and Pearson Australia
(a division of Pearson Australia Group Pty Ltd).

ISBN 978 0 8388 3372 8

2014 2013 2012 2011
10 9 8 7 6 5 4 3 2

Printed in China (SWTC/02)

Acknowledgements
The author and publisher would like to thank the following for permission
to reproduce the copyright material in this book.

Illustrations
Lewis Chandler, p. 18

Photographs
Alamy, pp. 29, 30; Big Stock, cover, pp. 6 (all),11, 13 (middle left), 17, 22; Corbis,
pp. 13 (bottom right), 23; Getty Images, pp. 4, 8; Harcourt Index, p. 24;
Pearson Australia/Alice McBroom Photography, p. 21; Photos.com,
p. 13 (right); Shutter Stock, pp. 7, 13 (middle right), 16; The Photo Library,
pp. 5, 9, 10 (all), 12, 14, 15, 19, 20 (all), 26, 27; 123rf.com, p. 13 (left)

Every effort has been made to trace and acknowledge copyright. The author
and publisher welcome any information from people who believe they own
copyright material in this book.

CONTENTS

CHAPTER 1

Clues and Evidence

What happens after a crime is committed? First someone has to report the crime. Then detectives visit the crime scene. They search for clues and evidence that will help identify the criminal. They examine the evidence carefully. Then they look at all the evidence and any other information they have collected and try to solve the crime.

A criminal investigator takes photos at a crime scene.

Criminal investigators check for fingerprints.

Every criminal leaves something behind at the crime scene. It doesn't matter how careful the criminal is. It might be a fingerprint, a shoe print, or even a lip print! It might be a button, a scrap of paper, or a strand of hair. The criminal usually carries away something as well. Perhaps it's a scratch on the hand, some dirt on the bottom of a shoe, or a single fiber from the victim's clothing.

All of this evidence is taken to a crime lab, where scientists perform many tests. The tests help them analyze the evidence and think about who committed the crime. The results of these tests can be used to help convict a criminal. This process is called forensic science, or forensics.

CHAPTER 2

A Unique Identity

WHAT IS DNA?

DNA is found inside every cell of your body. It's like an instruction manual to make you the person that you are. Everyone's DNA is different. Your particular DNA determines what your nose looks like, what color eyes you have, and how big your feet are.

Each person's DNA determines what she or he looks like.

DNA testing has been used to identify victims of disasters, such as the Asian Tsunami in 2004.

An Indonesian city destroyed by the Asian Tsunami

Your DNA is in every part of you. It's in a single hair or even a flake of dead skin. Because everyone's DNA is different, scientists can compare two different samples of DNA and tell whether they come from the same person. For example, they can look at the DNA from a hair found at a crime scene. Then they can compare it with DNA from a suspect's blood. If the two samples match, this information can be used as evidence to help convict the suspect.

SNOWBALL THE CAT

PRINCE EDWARD ISLAND
· CANADA ·
1995

Two hikers were pushing their way through the woods when they stumbled on a shallow grave. They immediately understood what that meant and raced back to their car to call the police.

Seven months earlier, a woman named Shirley had disappeared. Police had found her car four days later. It was in the woods eight miles from her home, and there were bloodstains on the seats.

Police found Shirley's car in the woods.

Police analyze DNA samples like this one to tie a suspect to a crime.

Now police asked forensic scientists to compare the blood in the car with the body in the grave. The DNA matched! So police knew that the blood in the car belonged to Shirley. They just had to search for her killer.

The police already had a suspect in mind—Shirley's ex-boyfriend, Douglas. Douglas had been in trouble with the law before. He lived in the area. Of course, he denied having anything to do with the murder.

When police had originally searched Shirley's car, they had found a man's brown leather jacket. It also had bloodstains on it. They strongly believed that the jacket belonged to Douglas. But they had no evidence to prove it.

Then the police had a breakthrough. They sent the jacket to a crime lab. The officer in charge of the case asked the scientists at the lab to confirm that the blood belonged to Shirley. He also wanted them to check the jacket for evidence about the killer.

The lab scientist said that the blood definitely belonged to Shirley. Then he told the officer that he had also found twenty-seven long, white cat hairs on the jacket.

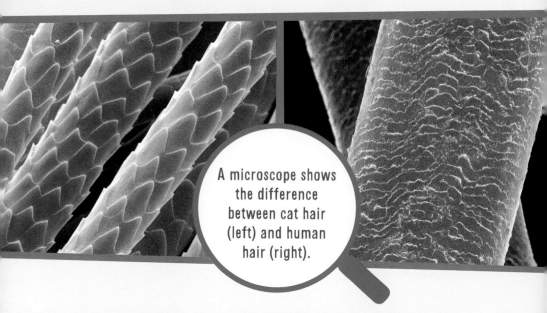

A microscope shows the difference between cat hair (left) and human hair (right).

At first, the officer was disappointed. He looked through his notes again. He was convinced he must have missed something. He pictured the visit he had made to Douglas's home. He remembered the furniture and where everyone had been sitting. Nothing was helpful.

Suddenly it came to him. A large, white cat named Snowball had been sitting on a chair in Douglas's living room.

The detectives returned to Douglas's home and took a blood sample from Snowball. They analyzed the cat's DNA in the crime lab. Then they compared it with the DNA of the cat hair found on the jacket. It was a match! Snowball's hair was on the murderer's jacket.

The police were finally able to prove that Douglas had murdered his ex-girlfriend. He was convicted and sentenced to life in prison. And all because of his cat!

CHAPTER 3

Leaving Your Mark

FINGERPRINTS

One of the first things investigators check for at a crime scene are fingerprints. People leave trails of oily or sweaty fingerprints wherever they go.

Fingerprints are easy to spot on dusty surfaces or on windows. But most prints are invisible. Police investigators check for these prints by dusting black powder over all the surfaces at a crime scene. Then they use special clear sticky tape to "lift" the prints from those surfaces. Sometimes they find prints by shining a laser on the surfaces. The prints glow in the powerful beam of light. With a laser, police sometimes find prints in places they may not have thought to look!

A police investigator uses black powder to dust for fingerprints.

FINGERPRINT TYPES

Everyone's fingerprints are slightly different. But all fingerprints can be grouped into different types. There are loops, arches, and whorls. There is also a type of print called a composite, which contains features of the other three types. Use a magnifying glass to look at your own fingertips. Which fingerprint type do you have?

Fingerprint types (left to right): an arch, a loop, a whorl, and a composite.

STUCK ON YOU

There's no way you can remove your fingerprints—you're stuck with them! The famous gangster John Dillinger was named Public Enemy Number 1 by the FBI in the 1930s. He didn't want to get caught, so he had a plastic surgeon remove his fingerprints. But they grew back. Next he tried burning them off with acid. They grew back again. He was finally caught in Chicago in November 1934.

FOOTPRINTS

Sometimes investigators find footprints or shoe prints at a crime scene. They photograph the prints and make molds of them.

Shoe prints can show what type of shoe the criminal was wearing and how big his or her feet are. They also give clues about the criminal's weight, height, and age.

An investigator makes a mold of shoe prints at a crime scene.

In some cases, investigators can even tell how fast people were moving. Footprints or shoe prints left by people who are running are farther apart and heavier than prints left by people who are walking. These prints can give information about how many people were in a particular place. They can also tell police which way the people were traveling and even the order in which events happened.

YOU BE THE JUDGE!

Police found shoe prints from a size 13 shoe at a crime scene. Who is most likely to have left them?

A a 90-year-old great-grandmother

B a tall teenage boy

C a petite, middle-aged businesswoman

(Answer below)

TIRE TRACKS

Tire tracks left at the scene of a crime can also be useful. Investigators study the tracks to find out the brand and age of the tires. Then they can figure out what kind of car was at the crime scene.

Sometimes dirt or mud from an unusual place is left in the tire tracks. Maybe the tracks show marks from tires that are very worn down on one side. People at the crime lab can analyze these clues to help identify the vehicle—and its owner.

Answer: B Size 13 is very large, and usually very large feet belong to tall people.

LIPS AND TEETH

The ridges on your lips, like your fingerprints, are also unique. Investigators check glasses and cups at crime scenes for lip prints. They also analyze any lipstick left behind to see if it matches the suspect's.

Your teeth are slightly different from everyone else's as well. Some people have big teeth. Others have crooked teeth. Some people are missing teeth or have gold fillings. Dentists keep a record of work they do on their patients' teeth. This record can be very useful to help identify accident or murder victims. But it can also be used to help catch criminals!

Investigators could analyze this glass for lipstick and lip prints.

Investigators could analyze the bite marks on this apple and compare them with dental records.

Have you ever chewed on a pencil? People leave bite marks on all kinds of things—foam drinking cups, bubble gum, and even half-eaten sandwiches or apples. Police investigators look at bite marks on items left behind at a crime scene. They can compare those marks with a suspect's dental records. If they find a match, it may help prove that the suspect was at the scene of the crime.

CHAPTER 4

Bits and Pieces

HAIR SAMPLES

People lose about one hundred hairs from their head each day. So it's not unusual to find hair at a crime scene. Hair comes in different colors—black, brown, blonde, red, and gray. Hair can be straight, curly, or wavy. Some people have very thick hair, while others have fine, or thin, hair.

Scientists can find out a great deal when they examine a hair under a microscope. They can tell if the hair came from a person's head, chin, or arm. They can also figure out if the hair comes from a person or an animal. They can examine the end of a piece of hair and decide whether the hair fell out naturally or was pulled out in a fight. They can even tell what kind of hair coloring or shampoo a suspect uses.

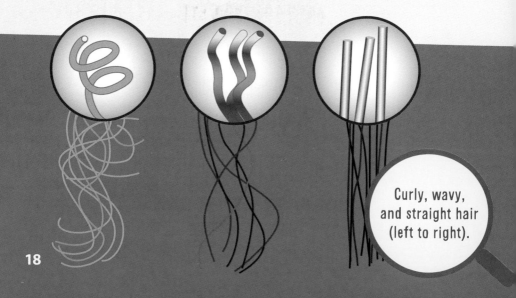

Curly, wavy, and straight hair (left to right).

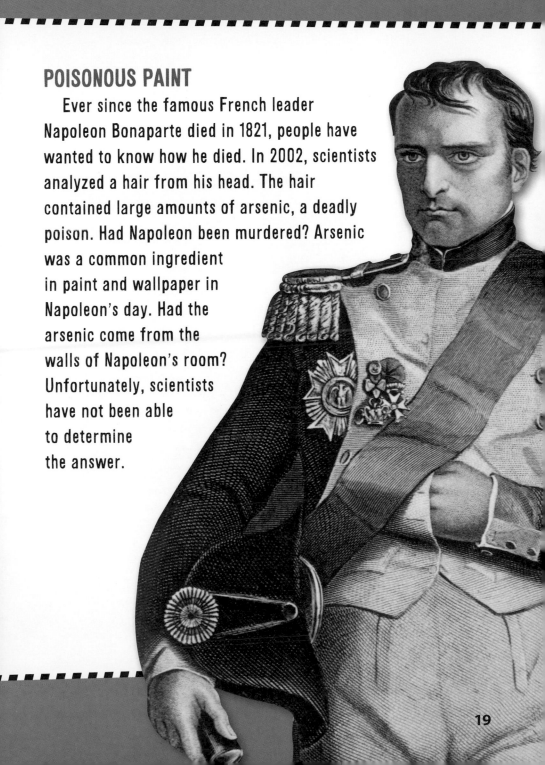

POISONOUS PAINT

Ever since the famous French leader Napoleon Bonaparte died in 1821, people have wanted to know how he died. In 2002, scientists analyzed a hair from his head. The hair contained large amounts of arsenic, a deadly poison. Had Napoleon been murdered? Arsenic was a common ingredient in paint and wallpaper in Napoleon's day. Had the arsenic come from the walls of Napoleon's room? Unfortunately, scientists have not been able to determine the answer.

FIBERS

Tiny fibers, or thin threads of material, fall from people's clothes all the time. The fibers land on furniture or on other people. Sometimes they land on other things, such as car seats.

These fibers can help link suspects to a crime. They can show a suspect has been in a particular place or in contact with a victim. Investigators use sticky tape to collect fibers from a crime scene. Then they take the fibers back to the crime lab to analyze them.

Wool, cotton, and nylon fibers (left to right) appear different under a microscope.

DIFFERENT FIBERS

WOOL

COTTON

NYLON

POLYESTER

TRY IT!

Use a piece of tape to remove fibers from several different kinds of fabric. Tape the fibers to a piece of white paper. Now examine them with a magnifying glass. Do they look different? How?

Many fibers that look very similar to the naked eye appear very different under a microscope. You can tell whether they are natural fibers, such as wool or cotton, or manufactured fibers, such as nylon. Some fibers have bumps and ridges, while others are smooth.

Some fibers are very unusual. They may have come from fabric that is very old or fabric that is only made in one part of the world. The fibers may have been colored with unusual dyes. If police can find the company that makes the fabric, sometimes they can find the criminals more easily.

CHAPTER 5

Trash—or Evidence?

Police often visit a suspect's home to search for clues. The first place they usually look is the trash can. Perhaps they'll find notes the criminal made about the crime. Maybe they will find crumpled bus or train tickets or airline boarding passes in the trash. These can show where the suspect was in the days just before, during, or after the crime.

The suspect's closet and washing machine are searched as well. They may contain clothing that was worn while the crime was being committed. The clothing is checked for bloodstains or fibers.

YOU BE THE JUDGE!

Jacob Williams lives next door to Joe's Burgers. Last week, his house was robbed. One of the suspects is Carl Weston. Police found a Joe's takeout container in Carl's trash can. Does this make him guilty of the crime?
(Answer below)

Answer: No, but it does place him near the scene of the crime.

Trash at the crime scene is also checked for clues. There may be fingerprints on a food container that has been thrown away. Scientists may even check the DNA on used pieces of bubble gum to see who chewed them.

If the crime took place in the victim's home, police check the contents of the victim's vacuum cleaner. Sometimes they contain hairs, dirt from a suspect's shoes, or fibers from a suspect's clothing. All of these clues can help link a suspect to a crime.

Investigators search the trash at a suspect's house.

CHAPTER 6

Handwriting Hints

Have you ever handed in a quiz without your name on it? Usually the teacher still knows whose quiz it is. That's because everyone's handwriting is different.

A handwritten note can give investigators information about the writer's age. It can also tell them whether the writer is right-handed or left-handed.

Handwriting experts check the shape of each letter and the spacing between the letters. They also look at how the letters slant and whether the letters have any special decorations, like circles or hearts that dot an "i." They check to see how far up a "t" is crossed and where the dot above an "i" appears. Sometimes the experts even check the back of the paper. This shows them how much force was used to push the pen into the paper.

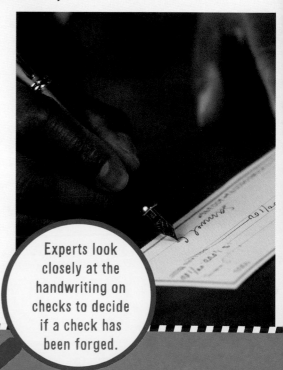

Experts look closely at the handwriting on checks to decide if a check has been forged.

YOU BE THE JUDGE!

One of these notes was written by an adult. The other two were written by kids. Which note was written by an adult? How can you tell? (Answer below)

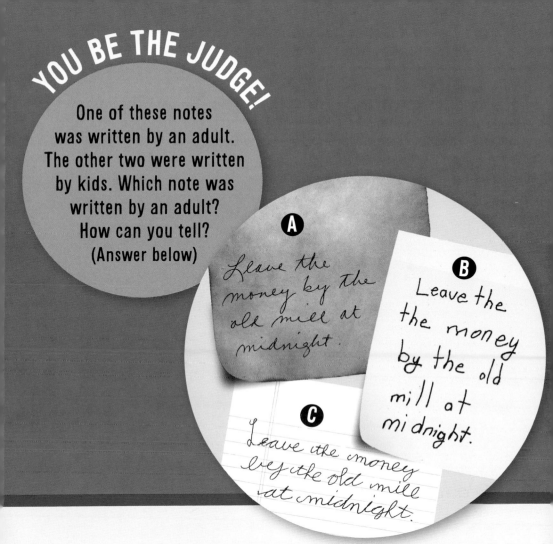

A Leave the money by the old mill at midnight.

B Leave the the money by the old mill at midnight.

C Leave the money by the old mill at midnight.

Handwriting experts can also compare two writing samples to see if the same person made them. This can be helpful to bankers who are trying to figure out if a check has been forged, or faked. It may help prove who wrote a ransom note in a kidnapping case.

Answer: A was written by an adult.

CHAPTER 7

Back at the Crime Lab

There are many different kinds of experts who work in the crime lab. Dentists study teeth and match them against dental records. Technicians use microscopes to examine hair and fiber samples. Their powerful microscopes can make a human hair appear 200 times larger than it actually is!

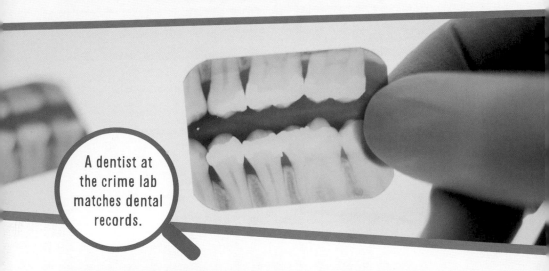

A dentist at the crime lab matches dental records.

Doctors called medical examiners examine bodies carefully. They try to find out how, when, or why a person died. This examination is called an autopsy. Sometimes tests show that the person was poisoned. Or maybe the person was hit on the head. Other times the tests show that the person died of natural causes, such as a heart attack.

Other scientists examine DNA samples and fingerprints. They enter everything they find in a national computer database. The database can help police match DNA and fingerprints of known criminals with those found at the scene of the crime.

Much of the evidence found at the crime scene is carefully labeled and stored at the crime lab. Sometimes crimes aren't solved right away, and the evidence can be held for years. One day, investigators might need the evidence to help solve the crime!

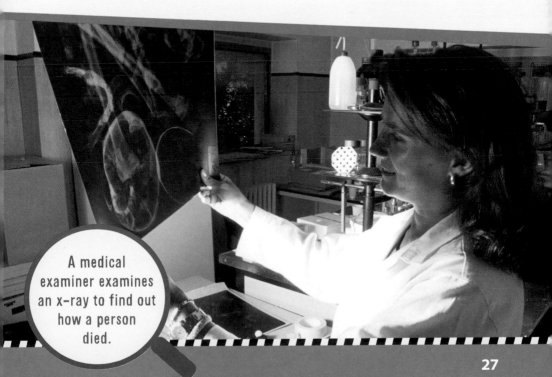

A medical examiner examines an x-ray to find out how a person died.

THE LAST MEAL

A man was driving home late one night when he saw a body on the side of the road. He quickly alerted the police. They searched the area but didn't find any clues. Police had no witnesses and no suspects. All they had was a woman's dead body.

Police brought the body to a medical examiner. A medical examiner tries to figure out how a victim died. One of the things a medical examiner checks is what's in the person's stomach. Usually they check the person's stomach to

determine if the victim was poisoned. This medical examiner didn't find any poison. But the examiner did find the victim's last meal: a taco. Tests showed the taco had been eaten only an hour before the victim died.

A police officer shows a photo of the victim to a witness.

Police visited every taco restaurant less than one hour's drive from where the victim had been found. They showed a picture of the victim to staff members at each restaurant. Finally, a waitress recognized the picture. The waitress told investigators that the woman had been in that restaurant. She had bought some tacos and then went to the café across the street.

A worker from the café also remembered the victim. He also knew the name of the man whom she had been talking with that night! The police rushed to his house. They found the victim's purse in the trunk of his car. The killer had been caught—by a taco!

BEYOND A REASONABLE DOUBT

Evidence from a crime scene is used in court when a suspect comes to trial. Technicians and medical officers sometimes appear in court as expert witnesses.

Technicians sometimes speak in court as expert witnesses.

Forensic science has made it much easier to prove that a suspect was at the scene of a crime or in contact with a victim. But forensic evidence, like DNA tests, can also prove that a suspect has *not* been involved in a crime. Sometimes this stops investigators from following the wrong trail. Other times, it can help set innocent people free.

Glossary

analyze	to study something scientifically
database	a collection of information stored on a computer
DNA	a basic material found in the cells of living things
evidence	something that provides proof
fiber	a thin thread of material
fingerprint	the mark left by the tip of a finger
forge	to make a fake or imitation
identical	exactly the same
laboratory	a place where scientific tests are carried out
laser	a beam of intense light
medical examiner	a doctor who tries to find out how someone died
microscope	a device that makes tiny objects look much larger
mold	a shape that liquid is poured into
suspect	someone the police think might have committed a crime
technician	a person who is an expert at a technical job
witness	a person who saw or heard something that happened

Index